ROBIN FORBES
A FIRST CAMERA BOOK

CLICK

MACMILLAN PUBLISHING CO., INC.
NEW YORK
COLLIER MACMILLAN PUBLISHERS
LONDON

With thanks to Eastman-Kodak Company for use of their
Kodak Instamatic X-15F and X-35F cameras.

Macmillan Publishing Co., Inc.
866 Third Avenue, New York, N.Y. 10022
Collier Macmillan Canada, Ltd.
Diagram on page 4 by Stephen M. Brown
Printed in the United States of America

10 9 8 7 6 5 4 3 2 1

Library of Congress Cataloging in Publication Data

Forbes, Robin.   Click, a first camera book.   Summary: Simple instructions for those
learning to handle a camera for the first time. 1. Photography—Juvenile literature.   [1. Photog-
raphy] I. Title.   TR149.F67   770'.282   78-31756   ISBN 0-02-735640-X
ISBN 0-02-043210-0 pbk.

Click: A First Camera Book is also available in a hardcover
edition from Macmillan Publishing Co., Inc.

To my goddaughter Caroline Nye,
and with many thanks for advice and encouragement
from Jerry Bragstad, David B. Eisendrath and Ann Morris.

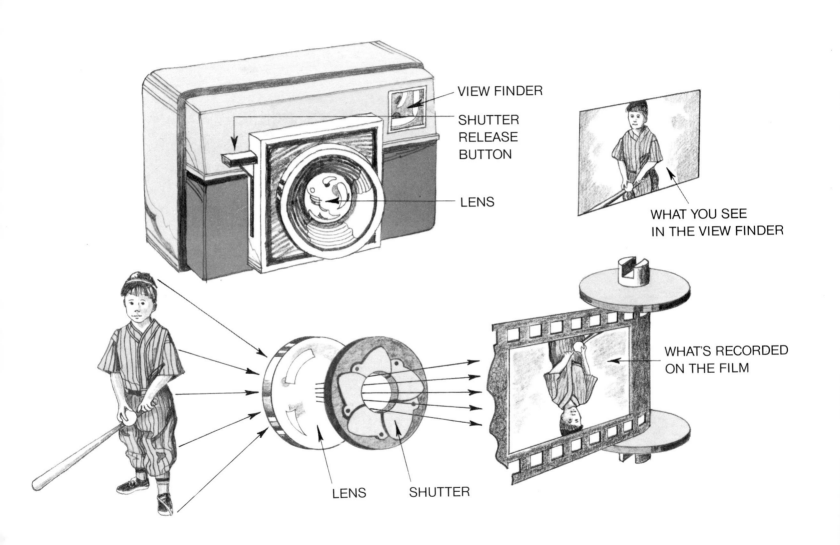

VIEW FINDER

SHUTTER RELEASE BUTTON

LENS

WHAT YOU SEE IN THE VIEW FINDER

WHAT'S RECORDED ON THE FILM

LENS

SHUTTER

The camera is a box that is light-tight. Light can only get in through an opening at one end. This opening is covered by a piece of glass or plastic, called a lens. As light passes through, the lens gathers it and makes it sharper.

There is a shutter in front of the lens. When you press the shutter release button, the shutter opens and closes very fast to let light in.

At the back of the camera is the film. Film is sensitive to light. When you point your camera at something, frame it in the view finder and press the shutter release button, the light reflected from whatever you are photographing enters the camera through the lens. The film is changed where the light hits it. When the film is taken out of the camera and treated with certain chemicals, the image of what you photographed will show on the film in reverse—in other words, what was dark shows as light and what was light shows as dark. A print is then made from this negative which has everything the right way round. The picture is just as you saw it in the view finder.

Before you take a picture, check to be sure there is film
in your camera. Don't open it up if you have film inside.
The counter will tell you how many pictures you have taken.

What do you see? Frame it in your camera.

Keep your fingers off the lens. Hold your camera just like this.

If you want to take the best picture, get in close. Don't stand
so far away! But remember that a simple camera won't take a sharp
picture closer than four feet.

Keep very still. If you move when you take your picture, it will be
fuzzy. Sometimes it helps to hold your breath before you press
the shutter button. Be sure and steady. Try to tuck your elbows in.
It might help to lean against a wall, or a table, or a tree.

Be quick to catch it, or be slow and patient.

Think about what you really see. Don't include too much.
What's really important in this picture?

Try to frame your picture.
Make sure your subject is in the middle,
not far off on the sides.

You may want to take your picture from up high or very low. Learn to bend! Sometimes that makes it more interesting.

When you photograph,
think about light.

There is front light,

back light,

side light

and even speckled light.

NOON

The best time to photograph anyone or anything
is morning or late afternoon, when the sun is not
directly overhead.

AFTERNOON

If you look carefully at light, you will also see shadows.
Shadows are caused by light.

How about shadows?

Sometimes there isn't enough light to take your picture.
Maybe you want to photograph someone indoors. You need
a flash cube. A flash adds light. Put the cube in the top
of your camera, and when you press the shutter button,
there will be a flash.

When you use a flash, make certain you aren't too close
(four feet) or too far away (eight feet).

Want to photograph people?
Your friends will love it when
you take their picture.

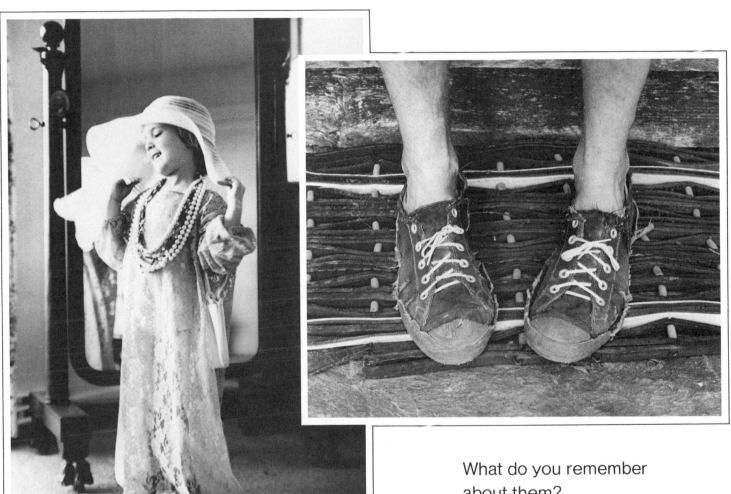

What do you remember
about them?

If you photograph people, watch out for trees, street lights
and telephone poles. Keep your background simple.

Are you shy? You can photograph
people all kinds of ways.

Sometimes it's good to ask people if you
can take their picture, but let them
go on with what they're doing.
Don't ask them to stop and look at you.

Watch out for too much glare because everyone squints in direct light. Watch out for shadows under your subject's eyes, too.

You can always ask your subject to move where
the light is better.

There are all sorts of things
to photograph. What in particular
catches your eye?

It's fun to photograph patterns
and shapes. Look around you!

Look for the same kinds
of patterns and shapes.

How about photographing things
that are white?

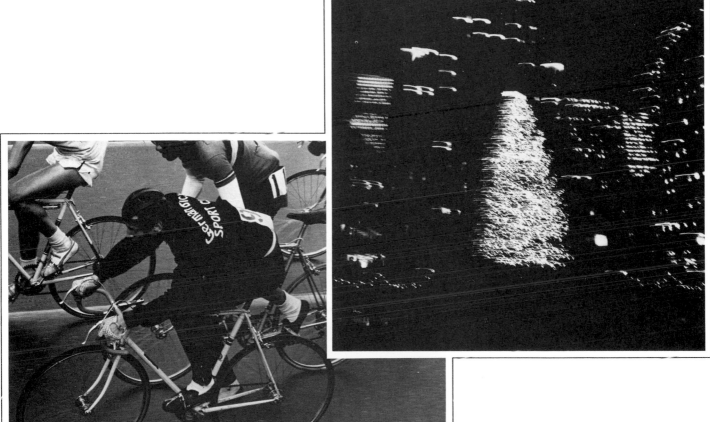

Or photograph black.

Some of the nicest things to
photograph are gray.
You see them all the time.

You can show different times of year in your photos, too—

spring, summer, fall, winter.

You can photograph anything you like—
but you can't photograph everything.
Choose what you really like, those
things you see that are special.

Everyone sees things differently and photographs things differently.
What you photograph says something about you as well as about
what you see.